Forests for Animals and Plants

The rainforest

This is the rainforest.

2

Many plants and animals live in the rainforest.

Plants and animals live here.

Plants and animals live here.

Plants and animals live here too.

4

5

Plants in the rainforest

Look at this plant.

It has very big **leaves**.

Big leaves help the plant to find the sun.

Look at this plant.

This plant grows on other plants in the rainforest.

Animals in the rainforest

Frogs live in the rainforest.

This frog is in the water.

It can find food

in the water.

Birds live in the rainforest.
These birds are in a **hole**
in the tree.

They are **safe**

in the tree.

13

Look at the kangaroo.
The kangaroo lives
in the trees.